How to Raise and Train a
BEAGLE

By
Mary Alice Ward and Sara M. Barbaresi

Distributed in the U.S.A. by T.F.H. Publications, Inc., 211 West Sylvania Avenue, P.O. Box 27, Neptune City, N.J. 07753; in England by T.F.H. (Gt. Britain) Ltd., 13 Nutley Lane, Reigate, Surrey; in Canada to the book store and library trade by Clarke, Irwin & Company, Clarwin House, 791 St. Clair Avenue West, Toronto 10, Ontario; in Canada to the pet trade by Rolf C. Hagen Ltd., 3225 Sartelon Street, Montreal 382, Quebec; in Southeast Asia by Y.W. Ong, 9 Lorong 36 Geylang, Singapore 14; in Australia and the south Pacific by Pet Imports Pty. Ltd., P.O. Box 149, Brookvale 2100, N.S.W., Australia. Published by T.F.H. Publications Inc. Ltd., The British Crown Colony of Hong Kong.

Y0-AIP-380

ACKNOWLEDGMENTS

Mr. Al Barry of Three Lions, Inc., photographed the Beagles of Marywards Kennels, owned by Mary Alice Ward and Louise M. Hoe, Belmont Avenue North, North Babylon, New York.

The illustrations by Paul Brown on page 8 and in the Appendix are reproduced by courtesy of the Gaines Dog Research Center, New York.

ISBN 0-87666-242-4

© Copyright 1958
by Sterling Publishing Co., Inc.

Contents

1. BEAGLE STANDARDS 5
   History of the Breed . . . Breed Specifications

2. BUYING YOUR BEAGLE 10
   Pet or Show Dog? . . . Male or Female? . . . Adult or Pup? . . . Where to Buy . . . What to Look for in a Puppy . . . Papers

3. CARE OF THE BEAGLE PUPPY 16
   Bringing Your Puppy Home . . . The Puppy's Bed . . . Feeding Your Puppy . . . Housebreaking Your Puppy . . . Veterinary Care . . . Worming . . . The Female Puppy

4. CARING FOR YOUR ADULT BEAGLE 23
   Diet . . . . Cleanliness and Grooming . . . Nose, Teeth, Ears and Eyes . . . Toenails . . . Parasites . . . First Aid . . . The Old Dog

5. HOW TO TRAIN YOUR BEAGLE 32
   Giving Commands . . . Lessons . . . Collar and Leash . . . Heeling . . . Teaching Your Dog to Come, Sit, Stay and Lie Down . . . Discipline and Training . . . Tricks . . . Retrieving . . . Field Training

6. CARING FOR THE FEMALE AND RAISING PUPPIES 47
   When to Breed . . . Choosing the Stud . . . Preparation for Breeding . . . The Female in Whelp . . . Preparing for the Puppies . . . Whelping . . . Raising the Puppies . . . Weaning the Puppies

7. SHOWING YOUR BEAGLE 54
   Advance Preparation . . . The Show

APPENDIX 59

The friendly Beagle deserves his great popularity as a pet and hunting dog.

1. Beagle Standards

With sad, soulful eyes and a merrily wagging tail, the Beagle is, it would seem, a paradox. In reality he is the friendliest, most patient and gentle of dogs, and certainly deserves his popularity.

Indeed he is popular. You will find Beagles in city apartments and suburban yards as well as in their "natural" home, the open country near rabbit burrows and woods with squirrels, foxes, and other wildlife. Probably the great majority of the many Beagles in this country are used for hunting each fall by their sportsmen owners. During the rest of the year they serve equally well as family pets and companions. Of course some Beagles are kept only as pets, and many appear in show and obedience trial rings.

HISTORY OF THE BREED

The Beagle is descended from English hounds of the time of Henry VIII. From these hounds also have come all the various breeds used to hunt in packs: Foxhounds, Harriers, Coon-, Otter-, Deer- and Wolfhounds. The Beagle is probably most like the original type of hound that has been traced back in literature and art to France of the Crusades, and even to ancient Greece.

Before 1800 two extreme types of Beagles were developed: a slow, deep-voiced Southern hound and his nimble Northern cousin. They ranged from six inches to nearly two feet tall. The modern Beagle owes much to a sporting parson of Essex, England, Reverend Honeywood, who assembled a uniform pack with characteristics midway between the Northern and Southern types. Today's hounds often trace their origin to them. In the United States a century ago there were many hunting dogs called Beagles. They were noted for their ability and stamina, but were lacking in looks. Imports from England in the '80s and '90s remedied this fault, but the breed was still used chiefly for hunting.

A group of well-to-do sportsmen promoted the breed and, in 1888, formed the National Beagle Club to hold pack field trials as well as bench shows. Several dozen recognized packs held frequent meets, hunting hare and cottontail rabbits with staff and hunt liveries.

Today Beagling in the United States is not an exclusive sport. There are several hundred Beagle clubs whose members keep a hound or two and enjoy hunting them themselves as well as running them in field trials, which are held almost every weekend throughout the fall and spring. Young and old alike train their own hounds and compete with their neighbors in friendly sport, the minor leagues of field trials leading to national and international competitions where more is at stake.

The Beagle imported from England nearly a hundred years ago was a fairly large dog, used mostly for fox-hunting over there, but selective breeding has brought the size down, with many Beagles no larger than 10 to 12 inches high. There are two size divisions which are judged separately in both shows and field trials: under 13″ and 13-15″, with 15″ high at the shoulders the maximum size allowable.

A variety of colors is seen in Beagles, with "any true hound color" allowed in the standard. Most common is black, tan and white, with black saddle over the back, shading into tan, with white legs, tail tip and throat, and often a white blaze, collar and underparts. The dog may be almost entirely tan with little black or white; more black; or white with only small colored spots. The large, dark eyes and floppy ears and high-carried tail are characteristic.

The Beagle under 13″ may weigh as little as 15 pounds, while his brother approaching the maximum 15″ will weigh up to 30 pounds in good, hard condition. An eager hunter who can run all day when properly conditioned, the Beagle will still be a quiet, lovable house dog, content to be exercised on leash and to obey your every command at home.

BREED SPECIFICATIONS

The standard by which the Beagle is judged, drawn up by the National Beagle Club (Morgan Wing, Jr., secretary, Millbrook, N. Y.) and approved by the American Kennel Club, follows:

HEAD—The skull should be fairly long, slightly domed at occiput [back of skull], with cranium broad and full.

EARS—Ears set on moderately low, long, reaching when drawn out nearly, if not quite, to the end of the nose; fine in texture, fairly broad—with almost entire absence of erectile power—setting close to the head, with the forward edge slightly inturning to the cheek—rounded at tip.

EYES—Eyes large, set well apart—soft and houndlike—expression gentle and pleading; of a brown or hazel color.

MUZZLE—Muzzle of medium length—straight and square cut—the stop moderately defined.

JAWS—Level. Lips free from flews; nostrils large and open.

Defects: A very flat skull, narrow across the top; excess of dome, eyes small, sharp and terrier-like, or prominent and protruding; muzzle long, snipey or cut away decidedly below the eyes, or very short. Roman nosed or upturned, giving a dish-faced expression. Ears short, set on high, or with a tendency to rise above the point of origin.

Ready for the hunt or show ring, this handsome Beagle, Ch. Marywards Mr. Long Island, is alert and poised on his toes.

BODY—NECK AND THROAT: Neck rising free and light from the shoulders, strong in substance yet not loaded, of medium length. The throat clean and free from folds of skin; a slight wrinkle below the angle of the jaw, however, may be allowable.

Defects: A thick, short, cloddy neck carried on a line with the top of the shoulders. Throat showing dewlap and folds of skin to a degree termed "throatiness."

SHOULDERS AND CHEST—Shoulder sloping—clean, muscular, not heavy or loaded—conveying the idea of freedom of action with activity and

This profile shows the Beagle's long skull, low-set, fairly broad ears, straight and square muzzle, and level jaws.

strength. Chest deep and broad, but not broad enough to interfere with the free play of the shoulders.

Defects: Straight, upright shoulders. Chest disproportionately wide or with lack of depth.

BACK, LOIN AND RIBS—Back short, muscular and strong. Loin broad and slightly arched, and ribs well sprung, giving abundance of lung room.

Defects: Very long or swayed or roached back. Flat, narrow loin. Flat ribs.

FORELEGS AND FEET—Forelegs straight, with plenty of bone in proportion to size of hound. Pasterns short and straight. Feet: Close, round and firm. Pad full and hard.

Defects: Out at elbows. Knees knuckled over forward or bent backward. Forelegs crooked or Dachshundlike. Feet long, open or spreading.

HIPS, THIGHS, HINDLEGS AND FEET—Hips and thighs strong and well muscled, giving abundance of propelling power. Stifles strong and well let down. Hocks firm, symmetrical and moderately bent. Feet close and firm.

Defects: Cowhocks or straight hocks. Lack of muscle and propelling power. Open feet.

TAIL—Set moderately high, carried gaily, but not turned forward over the back; with slight curve; short as compared with size of hound; with brush.

Defects: A long tail. Teapot curve or inclined forward from the root. Rat tail with absence of brush.

COAT—A close, hard, hound coat of medium length.

Defects: A thin, short coat, or of a soft quality.

HEIGHT—Height not to exceed 15 inches, measured across the shoulders at the highest point, the hound standing in a natural position with his feet well under him.

COLOR—Any true hound color.

GENERAL APPEARANCE—A miniature fox-hound, solid and big for his inches, with the wear-and-tear look of the hound that can last in the chase and follow his quarry to the death.

	Points	
Skull	5	
Ears	10	
Eyes	5	
Muzzle	5	
Head		25
Neck	5	
Chest and Shoulders	15	
Back, Loin and Ribs	15	
Body		35
Forelegs	10	
Hips, Thighs and Hindlegs	10	
Feet	10	
Running Gear		30
Coat	5	
Stern	5	
		10
Total		100

(Parts of the Beagle, and some common defects, are pictured in the Appendix, page 59.)

2. Buying Your Beagle

Perhaps you decided that you want a Beagle after seeing one of this merry breed. If you know someone whose Beagle has had puppies, it is a simple job to obtain one for yourself, but otherwise you must go out and look for him or her.

First, make up your mind what you want: male or female, adult or puppy, show dog or "just a pet." There is no greater use for a dog than being "just" a beloved pet and companion, but the dog which has profitable show and breeding possibilities is worth more to the seller.

PET OR SHOW DOG?

The puppy with a slight flaw in his ear carriage or quantity of coat will make just as good a companion and guardian, but his more perfect littermate will cost more.

That is why there is often a difference in price between puppies which look—to you, anyway—identical. If you think you may want to show your dog or raise a litter of puppies for the fun of it later on, by all means buy the best you can afford. You will save expense and disappointment later on. However, if the puppy is *strictly* a pet for the children, or companion for you, you can afford to look for a bargain. The pup which is not show material; the older pup, for which there is often less demand; or the grown dog, not up to being used for breeding, are occasionally available and are opportunities to save money. Remember that these are the only real bargains in buying a dog. It takes good food and care—and plenty of both—to raise a healthy, vigorous puppy.

The price you pay for your dog is little compared to the love and devotion he will return over the many years he'll be with you. With good care and affection your pup should live to a ripe old age; through modern veterinary science and nutrition, dogs are better cared for and living longer.

MALE OR FEMALE?

If you should intend breeding your dog in the future, by all means buy a female. You can find a suitable mate without difficulty when the time comes, and have the pleasure of raising a litter of pups—there is nothing cuter than a fat, playful puppy. If you don't want to raise puppies, your

These Beagle puppies are getting a good start in life and will soon be ready to go out to new homes.

female can be spayed, and will remain a healthy, lively pet. The female is smaller than the male and generally quieter. She has less tendency to roam in search of romance, but a properly trained male can be a charming pet, and has a certain difference in temperament that is appealing to many people. Male vs. female is chiefly a matter of personal choice.

ADULT OR PUP?

Whether to buy a grown dog or a small puppy is another question. It is undeniably fun to watch your dog grow all the way from a baby, sprawling and playful, to a mature, dignified dog. If you don't have the time to spend on the more frequent meals, housebreaking, and other training a puppy needs in order to become a dog you can be proud of, then choose an older, partly trained pup or a grown dog. If you want a show dog,

Look for a husky, healthy Beagle puppy like this when you choose your pet.

remember that no one, not even an expert, can predict with 100% accuracy what a small puppy will be when he grows up. Someone familiar with dogs may be right *most* of the time, but six months is the earliest age for the would-be exhibitor to pick a prospect and know that his future is relatively safe.

If you have a small child it is best to get a puppy big enough to protect himself, one not less than four or five months old. Older children will enjoy playing with and helping to take care of a baby pup, but at less than four months a puppy wants to do little but eat and sleep, and he must be protected from teasing and overtiring. You cannot expect a very young child to understand that a puppy is a fragile living being; to the youngster he is a toy like a stuffed dog.

WHERE TO BUY

You can choose among several places to buy your dog. One is a kennel which breeds show dogs as a business and has extra pups for sale as pets. Another is the one-dog owner who wants to sell the puppies from an occasional litter and thus pay his expenses. Pet shops usually buy puppies from overstocked kennels or part-time hobbyists for re-sale, and you can generally buy a puppy there at a reasonable price. To find any of these, watch the pet column of your local newspaper or look in the classified section of your phone book. If you or your friends go driving out in the countryside, be on the lookout for a sign announcing purebred puppies for sale.

Whichever source you try, you can usually tell in a very short time whether the puppies will make healthy and happy pets. If they are clean, fat and lively, they are probably in good health. At the breeder's you will have the advantage of seeing the puppies' mother and perhaps the father and other relatives. Remember that the mother, having just raised a demanding family, won't be looking her best, but if she is sturdy, friendly and well-mannered, her puppies should be, too. If you feel that something is lacking in the care or condition of the dogs, it is better to look elsewhere than to buy hastily and regret it afterward.

You may be impatient to bring home your new dog, but a few days will make little difference in his life with you. Often it is a good idea to choose a puppy and put a deposit on him, but wait to take him home until you have prepared for the new arrival. For instance, it is better for the Christmas puppy to be settled in his new home before the holidays, or else to wait until things have settled down afterward. You may want to wait until the puppy has completed his "shots," and if this is arranged in advance, it is generally agreeable.

If you cannot find the dog you want locally, write to the A.K.C. (page 15), for names of breeders near you, or to whom you can write for information. Puppies are often bought by mail from reputable breeders.

WHAT TO LOOK FOR IN A PUPPY

In choosing your puppy, assuming that it comes from healthy, well-bred parents, look for one that is friendly and outgoing. The biggest pup in the litter is apt to be somewhat overgrown or clumsy as a grown dog, while the appealing "poor little runt" may turn out to be a timid shadow—or have a Napoleon complex! If you want a show dog and have no experience in choosing the prospect, study the standard (page 6), but be advised by the breeder on the finer points of conformation. His prices will be in accord with the puppies' expected worth, and he will be honest with you because it is to his own advantage. He wants his good puppies placed in the public eye to reflect glory on him—and to attract future buyers.

The puppy should have bright eyes, without too much haw, or inner eyelid showing in the corner. His muzzle should be square, with big nostrils,

Proper cleaning, heating and feeding are marks of a good pet shop. If the puppies run from people, they have probably been mistreated. They should come up to the doors of the cage when you approach. The Beagle you choose should not be weak-looking or have running eyes.

and his whole head should be fairly long and evenly balanced. Ears should be low set, long and silky in feel, and should not rise when the dog shows interest. The neck should be quite long and clean of loose skin under the chin, although the puppy's skin all over should be loose and silky, with the hair soft and healthy-feeling. The body should be short and strong with deep chest and well-rounded ribs. The puppy may appear on the thin side because he is growing fast and has not as yet much muscle, but ribs and leg bones should not be too prominent. The chest should already be broad and legs should be straight, not bowed, with no sign of weakness. The puppy should stand on his toes, with neat feet. Although he will gambol and may wobble a bit from gawkiness when he moves, he should step out briskly and not meander or cross his feet when he trots.

PAPERS

When you buy your puppy you should receive his pedigree and registration certificate or application. These have nothing to do with licensing, which is a local regulation applying to purebred and mongrel alike. Find out the local ordinance in regard to age, etc., buy a license, and keep it on your dog whenever he is off your property.

Your dog's pedigree is a chart, for your information only, showing his ancestry. It is not part of his official papers. The registration certificate is the important part. If the dog was named and registered by his breeders you will want to complete the transfer and send it, with the fee of $1.00, to the American Kennel Club, 221 Fourth Ave., New York 3, N. Y. They will transfer the dog to your ownership in their records, and send a new certificate to you.

If you receive, instead, an application for registration, you should fill it out, choosing a name for your pup, and mail it with the fee of $2.00 to the A.K.C. Be sure that the number of the puppy's litter is included.

3. Care of the Beagle Puppy

BRINGING YOUR PUPPY HOME

When you bring your puppy home, remember that he is used to the peace and relative calm of a life of sleeping, eating and playing with his brothers and sisters. The trip away from all this is an adventure in itself, and so is adapting to a new home. So let him take it easy for awhile. Don't let the whole neighborhood pat and poke him at one time. Be particularly careful when children want to handle him, for they cannot understand the difference between the delicate living puppy and the toy dog they play with and maul. If the puppy is to grow up loving children and taking care of them, he must not get a bad first impression.

THE PUPPY'S BED

It is up to you to decide where the puppy will sleep. Unless it is winter in a cold climate, even a young puppy can sleep outside in a snug, well-built dog house. It should have a tight, pitched roof to let the rain run off, and a floor off the ground, to avoid dampness. The door should be no larger than the grown dog will need to go in and out, as a bigger opening lets in too much draft. For bedding you can use an old rag or blanket, straw, or sweet-smelling cedar shavings. Whether the puppy sleeps indoors or out, he will benefit from an outdoor run of his own where he can be put to exercise and amuse himself. It does not have to be large for if he goes for walks and plays with you he will get enough exercise that way. He is much safer shut in his run than being left loose to follow a stray dog off your property and get into bad habits—if he isn't hit by a car first!

Of course if the dog is left in his run for any length of time he should have protection from the cold, rain or sun. The run should be rectangular, and as big as you can conveniently make it, up to 20 x 40 feet, with strong wire fence which will keep your dog in and intruders out. The wire should be at least four feet high, as many dogs like to jump, and the gate should be fastened with a spring hook or hasp which is not likely to be unfastened by mischance.

If your dog sleeps indoors, he should have his own place, and not be allowed to climb all óver the furniture. He should sleep out of drafts, but not right next to the heat, which would make him too sensitive to the cold when he goes outside. If your youngster wants to share his bed with the puppy, that is all right, too, but the puppy must learn the difference between his bed and other furniture. Or he may sleep on a dog bed or in a box big enough to curl up in: a regulation dog crate or one made from a packing box, with bedding for comfort. If your cellar is dry and fairly warm the puppy will be all right there, or in the garage.

You have already decided where the puppy will sleep before you bring him home. Let him stay there, or in the corner he will soon learn is "his," most of the time, so that he will gain a sense of security from the familiar. Give the puppy a little milk with bread and kibble in it when he arrives, but don't worry if he isn't hungry at first. He will soon develop an appetite when he grows accustomed to his surroundings. The first night the puppy may cry a bit from lonesomeness, but if he has an old blanket or rug to curl up in he will be cozy. In winter a hot water bottle will help replace the warmth of his littermates, or the ticking of a clock may provide company.

FEEDING YOUR PUPPY

It is best to use the feeding schedule to which the puppy is accustomed, and stick to it except when you feel you can modify or improve it. You will probably want to feed the puppy on one of the commercially prepared dog foods as a base, flavoring it with table scraps and probably a little meat and fat when you have them. Remember that the dog food companies have prepared their food so that it is a balanced ration in itself, and, indeed, many dogs are raised on dog food alone. If you try to change this balance too much you are likely to upset your pet's digestion, and the dog will not be as well fed in the long run. Either kibble or meal is a good basic food, and the most economical way to feed your dog.

Milk is good for puppies and some grown dogs like it. Big bones are fine to chew on, especially for teething puppies, but small bones such as chicken, chop or fish bones are always dangerous; they may splinter or stick in the digestive tract. Table scraps such a meat, fat, or vegetables will furnish variety and vitamins, but fried or starchy foods such as potatoes and beans will not be of much food value. Adding a tablespoonful of fat (lard or drippings) to the daily food will keep your puppy's skin healthy and make his coat shine.

Remember that all dogs are individuals. The amount that will keep your dog in good health is right for him, not the "rule-book" amount. A feeding chart to give you some idea of what the average puppy will eat follows:

WEANING TO 3 MONTHS: *A.M.*—½ cup of dog food, mixed with warm water. *Noon*—½ cup warm milk, with cereal, kibble or biscuits. *P.M.*—¼ cup dog food, 1 tbs. meat, 1 tbs. fat; scraps. *Bedtime*—½ cup warm milk, biscuit.

3-6 MONTHS: *A.M.*—1 cup dog meal or kibble mixed with water. *Noon*—½ cup milk, soft-boiled egg twice a week. *P.M.*—¾ cup meal as above.

Feed your puppy in his own bowl at regular times and in the same place. Give him the amount of food he needs to keep healthy, using the feeding chart as a guide.

      6 MONTHS-1 YEAR: *A.M.*—1 cup dog meal, or milk with kibble. *P.M.*—1 cup dog meal with ¼ lb. meat, fat, scraps.
      OVER 1 YEAR: *A.M.*—Half of evening meal if you prefer. *P.M.*—2 cups meal with ½ lb. meat.
      You can try a system of self-feeding instead of giving your puppy regular meals. This means keeping the dry meal or kibble in front of him all the time. If he is inclined to overeat, put out only the daily amount each morning. Otherwise you can leave a filled dish or pail (protected from the weather and insects if outside) where he can nibble at leisure.

HOUSEBREAKING YOUR PUPPY

As soon as you get your puppy you can begin to housebreak him but remember that you can't expect too much of him until he is five months old or so. A baby puppy just cannot control himself, so it is best to give him an opportunity to relieve himself before the need arises.

Don't let the puppy wander through the whole house; keep him in one or two rooms under your watchful eye. If he sleeps in the house and has been brought up on newspapers, keep a couple of pages handy on the floor. When he starts to whimper, puts his nose to the ground or runs around looking restless, take him to the paper before an "accident" occurs. After he has behaved, praise him and let him roam again. It is much better to teach him the right way than to punish him for misbehaving. Puppies are

If you housebreak your puppy to newspapers, place him there before he has a chance to make mistakes, and praise him when he behaves.

naturally clean and can be housebroken easily, given the chance. If a mistake should occur, and mistakes are bound to happen occasionally, wash the spot immediately with tepid water, followed by another rinse with water to which a few drops of vinegar have been added. A dog will return to the same place if there is any odor left, so it is important to remove all traces.

If your puppy sleeps outside, housebreaking will be even easier. Remember that the puppy has to relieve himself after meals and whenever he wakes up, as well as sometimes in between. So take him outside as soon as he shows signs of restlessness indoors, and stay with him until he has performed. Then praise and pat him, and bring him back inside as a reward. Since he is used to taking care of himself outdoors, he will not want to misbehave in the house, and will soon let you know when he wants to go out.

You can combine indoor paper training and outdoor housebreaking by taking the puppy out when convenient and keeping newspaper available for use at other times. As the puppy grows older he will be able to control himself for longer periods. If he starts to misbehave in the house, without asking to go out first, scold him and take him out or to his paper. Punishment *after* the fact will accomplish nothing; the puppy cannot understand why he is being scolded unless it is immediate.

The older puppy or grown dog should be able to remain overnight in the house without needing to go out, unless he is ill. If your dog barks or acts restless, take him out once, but unless he relieves himself right away, take him back indoors and shut him in his quarters. No dog will soil his bed if he can avoid it, and your pet will learn to control himself overnight if he has to.

VETERINARY CARE

You will want your puppy to be protected against the most serious puppyhood diseases: distemper and infectious hepatitis. So your first action after getting him will be to take him to your veterinarian for his shots and a check-up, if he has not already received them. He may have had all or part of the immunization as early as two months of age, so check with the seller before you bring your puppy home.

You may give the puppy temporary serum which provides immunity for about two weeks, but nowadays permanent vaccine providing lifelong immunity can be given so early that the serum is seldom used, except as a precaution in outbreaks. The new vaccine is a combined prevention against distemper and hepatitis, and may be given in one or three shots (two weeks apart). Your veterinarian probably has a preferred type, so go along with him, as either method is protective in a very high percentage of cases.

There is now an effective anti-rabies vaccine, which you can give to your dog if there should be an outbreak of this disease in your neighborhood. It is not permanent, however, so unless local regulations demand it, there is little value in giving the vaccine in ordinary circumstances.

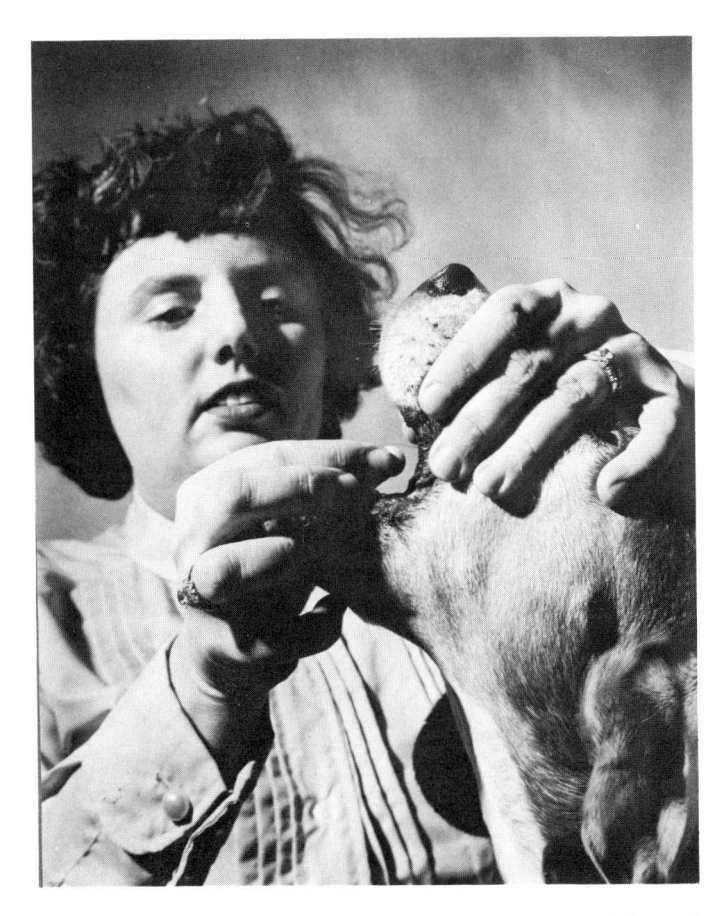

When you have to give your dog a pill, hold his mouth closed until he swallows.

WORMING

Your puppy has probably been wormed at least once, since puppies have a way of picking up worms, particularly in a kennel where they are exposed to other dogs. Find out when he was last wormed and the date, if any, for re-worming. Older dogs are usually able to throw off worms if they are in good condition when infected, but unless the puppy is given some help when he gets worms, he is likely to become seriously sick. New worm medicines containing the non-toxic but effective piperazines may be bought at your pet store or druggist's, and you can give them yourself. But remember to follow instructions carefully and do not worm the puppy unless you are sure he has worms.

If the puppy passes a long, string-like white worm in his stool or coughs one up, that is sufficient evidence, and you should proceed to worm him. Other indications are: general listlessness, a large belly, dull coat, mattery eye and coughing, but these could also be signs that your puppy is coming down with some disease. If you only *suspect* that he has worms, take him to your veterinarian for a check-up and stool examination before worming.

THE FEMALE PUPPY

If you want to spay your female you can have it done while she is still a puppy. Her first seasonal period may occur as early as nine months. She may be spayed before or after this, or you may breed her and still spay her afterward.

The first sign of the female's being in season is a thin red discharge, which will increase for about a week, when it changes color to a thin yellowish stain, lasting about another week. Simultaneously there is a swelling of the vulva, the dog's external sexual organ. The second week is the crucial period, when she could be bred if you want her to have puppies, but it is possible for the period to be shorter or longer, so it is best not to take unnecessary risks at any time. After a third week the swelling decreases and the period is over for about six months.

The female will probably lose her puppy coat, or at least shed out part of it, about three months after she is in season, for this is the time when her puppies would be weaned if she had been mated, and females generally drop coat at that time.

If you have an absolutely climb-proof and dig-proof run within your yard, it will be safe to leave her there, but otherwise the female in season should be shut indoors. Don't leave her out alone for even a minute; she should be exercised only on leash. If you want to prevent the neighborhood dogs from hanging around your doorstep, as they inevitably will as soon as they discover that your female is in season, take her some distance away from the house before you let her relieve herself. Take her in your car to a park or field for a chance to stretch her legs. After the three weeks are up you can let her out as before, with no worry that she can have puppies until the next season. But if you want to have her spayed, consult your veterinarian about the time and age at which he prefers to do it. With a young dog the operation is simple and after a night or two at the animal hospital she can be at home, wearing only a small bandage as a souvenir.

This Beagle is in excellent condition, neither too fat nor too thin. Good food and exercise will keep him healthy and help him live a long life.

4. Caring for Your Adult Beagle

DIET

When your dog reaches his first birthday he is no longer a puppy, although he will not be fully mature and developed until he is two. For all intents and purposes, however, he may be considered full grown and adult now.

You may prefer to continue feeding your dog twice a day, although he can now eat all that he needs to be healthy at one meal a day. Usually it is best to feed that one meal, or the main meal, in the evening. Most dogs

If your Beagle becomes used to being groomed and handled from puppyhood, he will enjoy it. A high bench makes grooming easy.

eat better this way, and digest their food better. If your dog skips an occasional meal, don't worry; after half an hour remove the food if he turns up his nose at it. Otherwise he will develop the habit of picking at his food, and food left out too long becomes stale or spoiled. If you use the dry self-feeding method, of course this does not apply.

The best indication of the correct amount to feed your dog is his state of health. A fat dog is not a healthy one; just like a fat person, he has to strain his heart—and his whole body—to carry excess weight. If you cannot give your dog more exercise, cut down on his food, and remember that those dog biscuits fed as snacks or rewards count in the calories. If your dog is thin, increase the amount and add a little more fat. You can also add flavoring he likes to pep up his appetite. The average grown dog needs

2 to 3 cups of dog meal, or a half-pound of canned food with an additional cup of meal per day. Use your own judgment for YOUR dog.

CLEANLINESS AND GROOMING

With his short coat, the Beagle needs little in the way of grooming. A weekly brushing will keep him in good condition.

You should establish good grooming habits while your dog is a young puppy. Even though his coat is short and does not need much brushing, the puppy should learn to stand for the operation, preferably on a bench or table. When he is full grown, brushing will be easier if the dog stands quietly at a convenient height. Equipment should include a soft brush and hound glove.

Your Beagle will seldom need a bath unless he gets into something smelly or is so dirty that brushing isn't enough. When you bathe him,

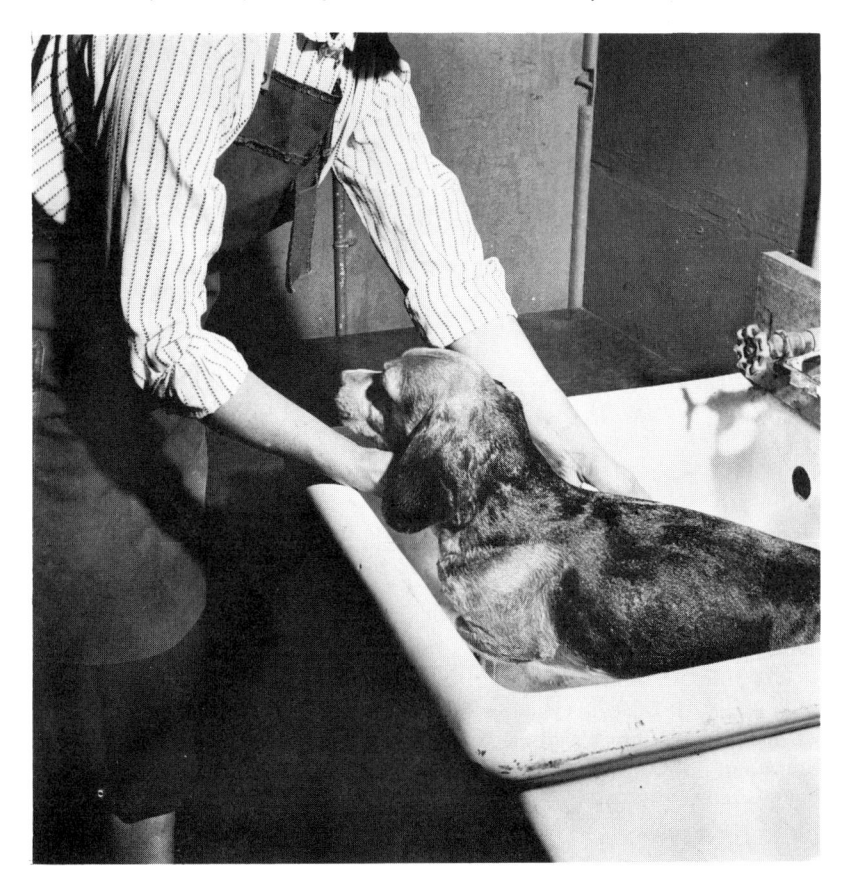

After you bathe your Beagle, be sure to rinse all the soap out of his coat.

Dry your Beagle thoroughly after his bath to prevent chills.

use one of the special dog soaps, a shampoo made for humans, or soap pieces dissolved to make a solution. Be sure to rinse all the soap out so no residue will be left to irritate the skin. Use towels to dry your Beagle afterward and, if the weather is cool, keep him in a warm place to prevent chilling. Too much bathing will dry the skin and cause shedding, so don't overdo it. If your Beagle likes to swim, he will get enough bathing that way in the summer.

If your dog's skin is dry or if he sheds more than a few hairs when groomed, it may be due to lack of fat in his diet. Add more bacon fat or lard to his food, increasing the amount of lard to two or three tablespoons. Other skin troubles, shown by scratching, redness, or a sore on the surface, should be examined by your veterinarian, who can prescribe treatment and clear up the trouble quickly. Don't delay, as once it takes hold any skin disease is hard to cure.

NOSE, TEETH, EARS AND EYES

Normally, a dog's nose, teeth, ears and eyes need no special care. The dog's nose is cool and moist to the touch (unless he has been in a warm house); however, the "cold nose" theory is only a partial indication of health or sickness. A fever, for instance, would be shown by a hot, dry nose, but other illness might not cause this. The dog's eyes are normally bright and alert, with the eyelid down in the corner, not over the eye. If the haw is bloodshot or partially covers the eye, it may be a sign of illness or irritation. If your dog has matter in the corners of the eyes, bathe with a mild eye wash; obtain ointment from your veterinarian or pet shop to treat a chronic condition.

If your dog seems to have something wrong with his ears which causes him to scratch them or shake his head, cautiously probe the ear with a cotton swab. An accumulation of wax will probably work itself out. But dirt or dried blood is indicative of ear mites or infection, and should be treated immediately. Sore ears in the summer, due to fly bites, should be

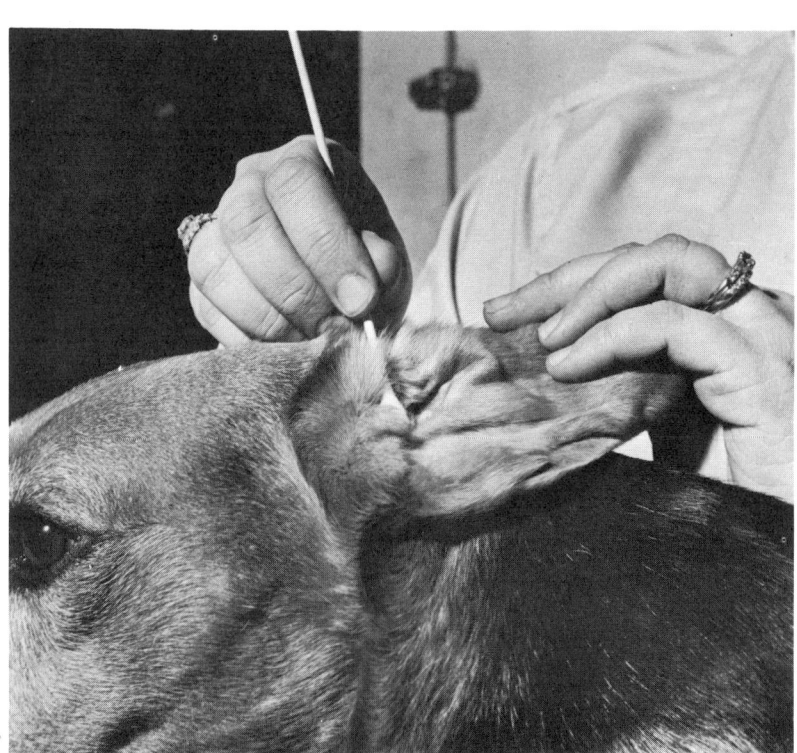

When you clean your dog's ears, use a cotton swab and probe gently.

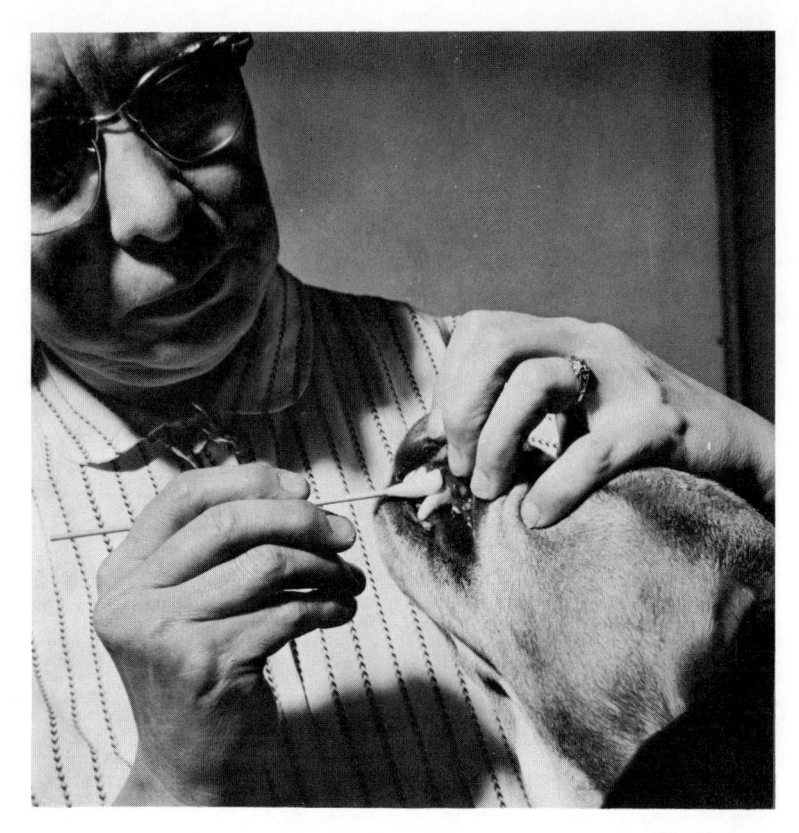

It is a good idea to have the tartar removed from your dog's teeth occasionally. Use a peroxide solution on a swab.

washed with mild soap and water, then covered with a soothing ointment, gauze-wrapped if necessary. Keep the dog protected from insects, and if necessary keep him indoors until his ears heal.

The dog's teeth will take care of themselves, although you may want your veterinarian to scrape off the unsightly tartar accumulation occasionally. A good hard bone will help to do the same thing.

TOENAILS

Keep your dog's toenails short with a weekly clipping. Use specially designed clippers that are available at your pet shop. Never take off too much at one time, as you might cut the "quick" which is sensitive and will bleed. Cut the nails straight across, then round off the sides with a little clip or a file. Be particularly careful when you cut black nails in which the quick is not visible.

PARASITES

If your dog picks up fleas or other skin parasites from neighbors' dogs or from the ground, weekly use of a good DDT- or Chlordane-base flea powder will get rid of them. Remember to dust his bed and change the bedding, too, as flea eggs drop off the host to hatch and wait in likely places for the dog to return. In warm weather a weekly dusting or monthly dip is good prevention.

If your grown dog is well-fed and in good health you will probably have no trouble with worms. He may pick them up from other dogs, however, so if you suspect worms, have a stool examination made and, if necessary, worm him. Fleas, too, are carriers of tapeworm, so that is one good reason to make sure the dog is free from these insects. Roundworms, the dog's most common intestinal parasite, have a life cycle which permits complete eradication by worming twice, ten days apart. The first worming will remove all adults and the second will destroy all subsequently hatched eggs before they in turn can produce more parasites.

Cut your dog's nails regularly if they are not worn down by normal exercise. Be sure that you don't cut too much at one time.

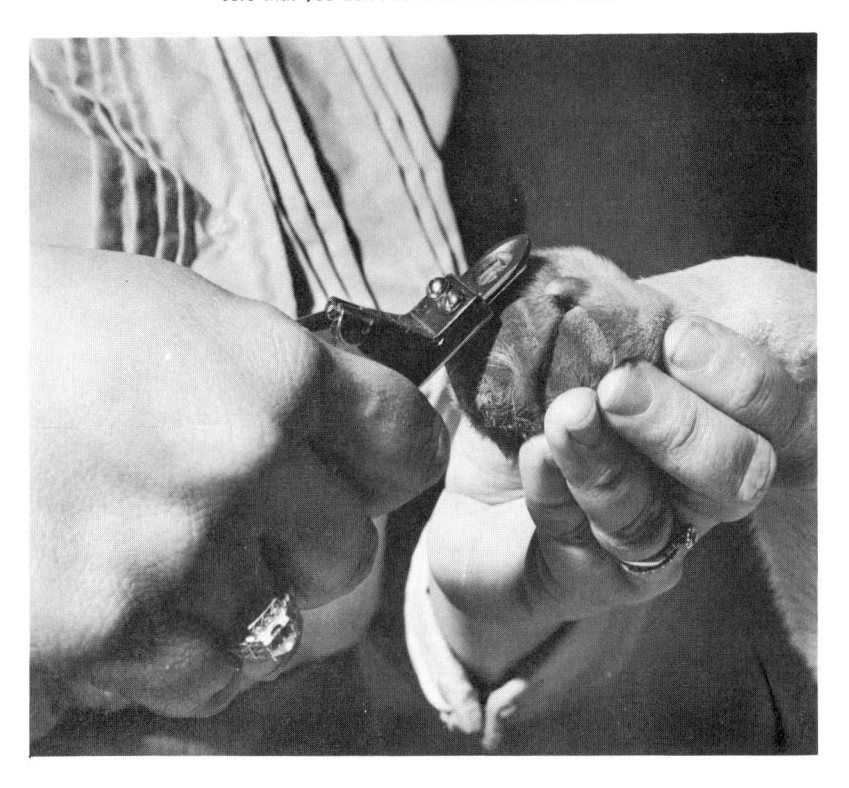

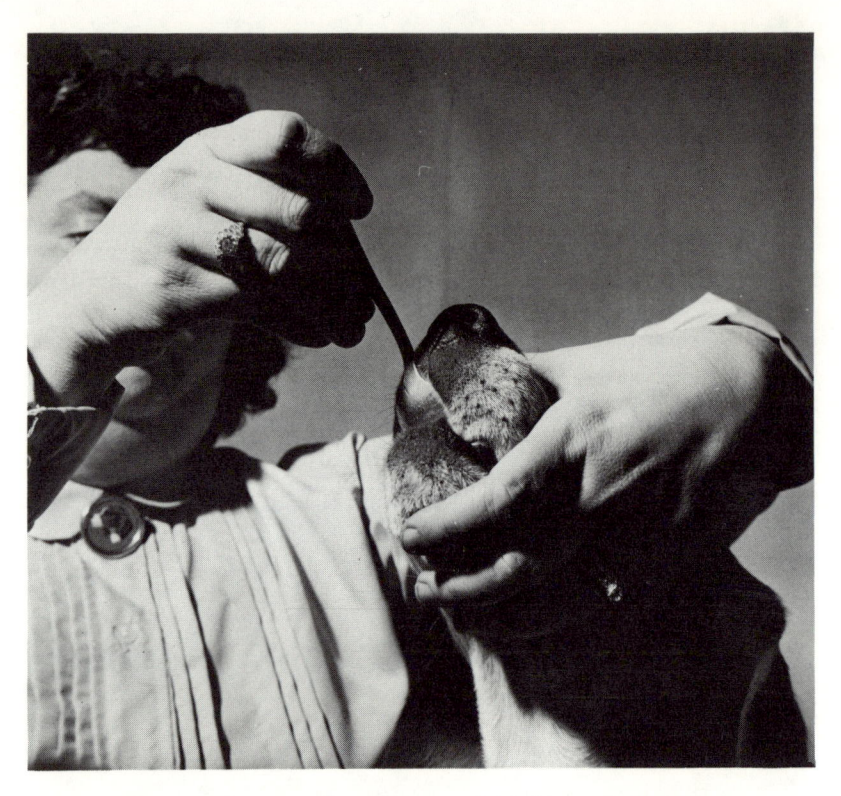

When your Beagle needs medicine, pour it into his mouth this way.

FIRST AID

If your dog is injured, you can give him first aid which is, in general, similar to that for a human. The same principles apply. Superficial wounds should be disinfected and healing ointment applied. If the cut is likely to get dirty apply a bandage and restrain the dog so that he won't keep trying to remove it. A cardboard ruff will prevent him from licking his chest or body. Nails can be taped down to prevent scratching.

A board splint should be put on before moving a dog that might have a broken bone. If you are afraid that the dog will bite from pain, use a bandage muzzle made from a long strip of cloth, wrapped around the muzzle, then tied under the jaw and brought up behind the ears to hold it on. In case of severe bleeding on a limb, apply a tourniquet—a strip of cloth wrapped around a stick to tighten it will do—between the cut and the heart, but loosen it every few minutes to avoid damaging the circulation.

THE OLD DOG

With the increased knowledge and care available, there is no reason why your dog should not live to a good old age. As he grows older he may need a little additional care, however. Remember that a fat dog is not healthy, particularly as he grows older, and limit his food accordingly. The older dog needs exercise as much as ever, although his heart cannot bear the strain of sudden and violent exertion. His digestion may not be as good as it was as a puppy, so follow your veterinarian's advice about special feeding, if necessary. Failing eyesight or hearing mean lessened awareness of dangers, so you must protect him more than before. The old dog is used to his home, and to set ways, so too many strangers are bound to be a strain. For the same reason, boarding him out or a trip to the vet's are to be avoided unless absolutely necessary.

Should you decide at this time to get a puppy, to avoid being without a dog when your old retainer is no longer with you, be very careful how you introduce the puppy. He is naturally playful and will expect the older dog to respond to his advances. Sometimes the old dog will get a new lease on life from a pup. But don't make him jealous by giving to the newcomer the attention that formerly was exclusively his. Feed them apart, and show the old dog that you still love him the most; the puppy, not being used to individual attention, will not mind sharing your love.

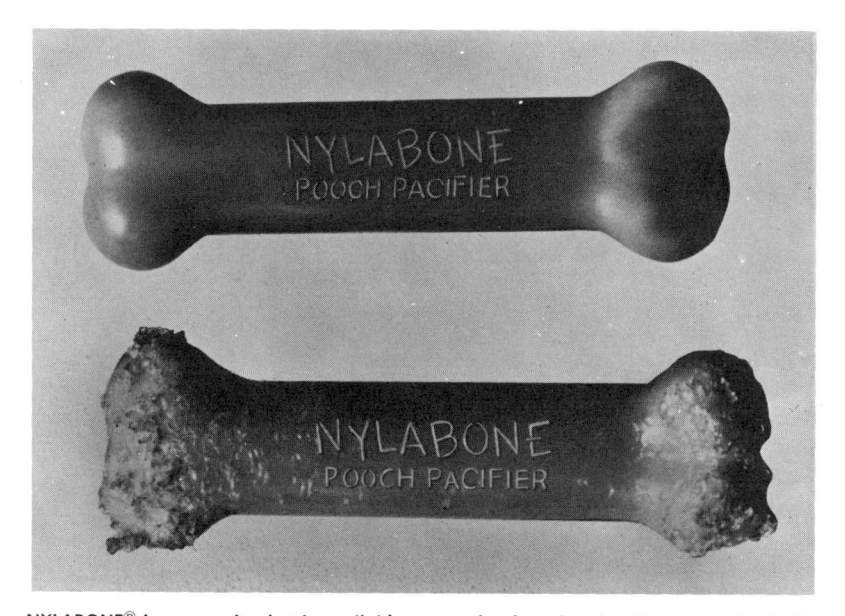

NYLABONE® is a necessity that is available at your local petshop (not in supermarkets). The puppy or grown dog chews the hambone flavored nylon into a frilly dog toothbrush, massaging his gums and cleaning his teeth as he plays. Veterinarians highly recommend this product . . . but beware of cheap imitations which might splinter or break.

5. How to Train Your Beagle

The Beagle may be easily trained to become a well-behaved member of your family. Training should begin the day you get him. Although a puppy under six months is too young for you to expect much in the way of obedience, you should teach him to respect your authority. Be consistent. Don't allow the pup to jump all over you when you are wearing old clothes, because you can't expect him to know the difference when you are dressed for a party. Don't encourage the dog to climb into your lap or onto your bed, then punish him for leaving hair on furniture when you aren't around. Although six months to a year is the best time to begin serious training, a dog of any age can learn if you use consideration and patience. You *can* teach an old dog new tricks.

Housebreaking has already been covered. You cannot expect perfection from a puppy, or even an older dog, particularly if he is not used to living in a house. A dog in a strange place is likely to be ill at ease and make a mistake for that reason. Remember that once this has happened, you can only prevent further accidents by not allowing the opportunity to arise. Be sure to remove all traces which would remind the dog of previous errors.

After you have taught your dog to be clean indoors and to relieve himself outside, you should teach him to do it on command, not only in one familiar place. It is a convenience when traveling to be able to keep him on leash, so take the time to teach him before it is necessary. "Curb your dog" is the rule in most cities; for the sake of others you should teach your dog to obey it.

GIVING COMMANDS

When you give commands use the shortest phrase possible and use the same word with the same meaning at all times. If you want to teach your dog to sit, then always use the word SIT. If you want your dog to lie down, then always use the word DOWN. It doesn't matter what word you use as long as your dog becomes accustomed to hearing it and acts upon it.

The trick dog that always sits on the command UP and stands at SIT was trained to obey the words that way, since words are merely sounds to him. Your dog does not understand what you say, but associates the word with his training and the tone of your voice. Unless you use commands consistently your dog will never learn to obey promptly.

If you begin to train your puppy the day you get him, and use patience and firmness, you will soon have a wonderful companion you can be proud of.

LESSONS

Try to make your training lessons interesting. Short, frequent lessons are of much more value than long ones occasionally. It is better to train your dog 10 minutes a day than 30 minutes once a week.

COLLAR AND LEASH

Your puppy should become used to a leash and collar at an early age. He seldom needs a license until he is six months old, and a leather collar will be outgrown several times before then. Buy one for use, not looks or permanence. A thin chain "choke collar" is a good substitute, but you will want a larger and slightly heavier one for training later on. Never leave a choke on a loose dog, for it could catch on something and strangle him. If you want to use one as a permanent collar, buy a clip to fasten the two ends, so that it cannot choke him.

Let the puppy wear his collar around until he is used to its feel and weight. After several short periods he will not be distracted by the strangeness and you can attach the leash. Let him pull it around and then try to lead him a bit. He will probably resist, bucking and balking, or simply sitting down and refusing to budge. Fight him for a few minutes, dragging him along if necessary, but then let him relax for the day, with plenty of affection and praise. He won't be lead-broken until he learns that he must obey the pull under any circumstance, but don't try to do it in one lesson. Ten minutes a day is long enough for any training. The dog's period of concentration is short and, like a child, he will become bored if you carry it on too long.

HEELING

Once the puppy obeys the pull of the leash half your training is accomplished. "Heeling" is a necessity for a well-behaved dog, so teach him to walk beside you, head even with your knee. Nothing looks sadder than a small dog taking his helpless owner for a walk. It is annoying to passers-by and other dog-owners to have a dog, however friendly, bear down on them and entangle dogs, people and packages.

To teach your dog, start off walking briskly, saying "Heel" in a firm voice. Pull back with a sharp jerk if he lunges ahead, and if he lags repeat the command and tug on the leash, not allowing him to drag behind. After the dog has learned to heel at various speeds on leash, you can remove it and practice heeling free, but have it ready to snap on again as soon as he wanders.

You must understand that most dogs like to stop and sniff around a bit until they find *the* place to do their duty. Be kind enough to stop and wait for your dog when he finds it necessary to pause.

The first step in training your Beagle is teaching him to walk freely on leash. If you give him plenty of praise, he will learn very quickly.

TEACHING YOUR DOG TO COME, SIT, STAY AND LIE DOWN

When the dog understands the pull of the leash he should learn to come. Never call him to you for punishment, or he will be quick to disobey. Always go to him if he has been disobedient. To teach him to come, let him reach the end of a long lead, then give the command, pulling him toward you at the same time. As soon as he associates the word "Come" with the action, pull only when he does not respond immediately. As he starts to come, back up to make him learn that he must come from a distance as well as when he is close to you. Soon you can practice without a leash, but if he is slow to come or actively disobedient, go to him and pull him toward you, repeating the command. More practice with leash on is needed.

When you and your dog are out walking, he should heel, with his head even with your left knee. After he has learned to heel on the leash, you can teach him to heel without it.

(Above) After your Beagle has learned to sit, teach him to stay in place.
(Below) Teach your Beagle to stay away from cars by discouraging him with a firm "No."

37

"Sit," "Down," and "Stay" are among the most useful commands and will make it easier for you to control your dog on many occasions—during grooming, veterinary care, walks when you meet a strange dog, drives in the car, and so forth. Teaching him to sit is the first step. With collar and leash on have him stand in the "Heel" position. Give the command "Sit," at the same time pulling up on the leash in your right hand and pressing down on his hindquarters with your left. As soon as he sits, release the pressure and praise him.

To teach your dog to stay, bring your hand close to his face with a direct motion at the same time as you give the order. Ask him to remain only a few seconds at first, but gradually the time can be increased and you can leave him at a distance. If he should move, return immediately and make him sit and stay again, after you scold him.

If you don't want dog hairs all over everything, train your Beagle to stay off the furniture.

Your Beagle will learn to stand on his hind legs and beg if you train him with patience.

To teach your dog to lie down, have him sit facing you. Pull down on the leash by putting your foot on it and pulling at the same time as you say "Down." Gesture toward the ground with a sweep of your arm. When he begins to understand what is wanted, do it without the leash and alternate voice and hand signals. Teach him to lie down from standing as well as sitting position, and begin to do it from a distance. Hand signals are particularly useful when your dog can see you but is too far away to hear, and they may be used in teaching all commands.

DISCIPLINE TRAINING

If you are consistent in your training and stop the puppy every time he starts to misbehave, he is not likely to get into bad habits. Every puppy

This handsome Beagle has the black, tan and white hound markings that are typical of the breed.

Ch. Gaycroft Chuckle poses proudly in front of some of his show awards.

goes through a teething period, but if he has his own toy or bone he won't chew up the furniture. If the puppy learns not to jump up, and to stay off the furniture, he will not pick up the habit later on. If you call him back to you or jerk his leash when he wants to chase a car or bicycle, he will soon learn that it is forbidden.

With a dog that has already acquired bad habits, stronger measures are needed. If he jumps on people, knock him off balance with a well-aimed knee, or step on his hind toes, *at the same time as you say "no."* You can cure him of chasing cars with a water pistol or a whole bucket of water dumped on his unsuspecting head. If you catch him in the act from behind you will also spoil his fun.

Prevention of all bad habits is easier than cure, and there is no reason why you cannot train your dog. There are many books on the subject in your local public library, and many towns have obedience training classes which hold weekly meetings with an experienced trainer to help you teach your dog. We strongly recommend taking your dog to class; the A.K.C. or Gaines Dog Research Center can supply a list of near-by classes.

TRICKS

Most dogs learn a few tricks without even trying. With patient training you can teach your dog to shake paws, roll over, sit up, beg, and do many other tricks.

To teach your Beagle to shake hands, first have him sit. Then, upon the command "Paw," lift his paw in your hand and shake it vigorously without knocking him off balance. Then give him a piece of dog candy. Repeat this several times a day and in a week he will all but hold out his paw when you walk in the door!

Teach him to beg in the same way. Have him sit, and, as you give the command "Beg," lift his front paws up until he is in a begging position. Hold him that way until he finds a comfortable balance; then let him balance himself, and hold a piece of dog candy over his nose. Release his paws, lower the candy to his mouth, and hold it firmly so he has to pry it loose. Repeat the command "Beg" over and over until he assumes the position upon the command. Reward him whenever he obeys.

RETRIEVING

Many Beagles are born retrievers. You can have fun throwing sticks or toys for your dog to fetch, but to teach him to do serious retrieving, place the object in his mouth at first, giving the command "Fetch." Then get him to take it from your hand, the ground, and finally throw it increasing distances. It will still be an amusing game for him, but he can be counted on to retrieve what you want.

This brace of Beagles is eager to be off hunting.

FIELD TRAINING

You can train your own Beagle for the field, because hunting comes naturally to him. He should already know the commands Come, Sit, Heel and Stay, and be quick to obey. The winning field trial Beagle, in tough competition, must be letter-perfect, but you can enjoy gunning with your dog if he is able to handle game — bring it within shooting range or follow it to its hole.

When your Beagle is still a puppy he may be ready for field training if he is quiet and obedient, but if he is excitable he will be hard to control, and it is better to wait until he has settled down. Many Beagles have become successful hunters when first introduced to the sport at three or four years of age.

(Above) A Beagle puppy makes a wonderful companion for a boy or girl. A youngster gains responsibility by taking care of his own dog.

(Below) A Beagle mother and her puppies enjoying life in a comfortable, well-bedded whelping box.

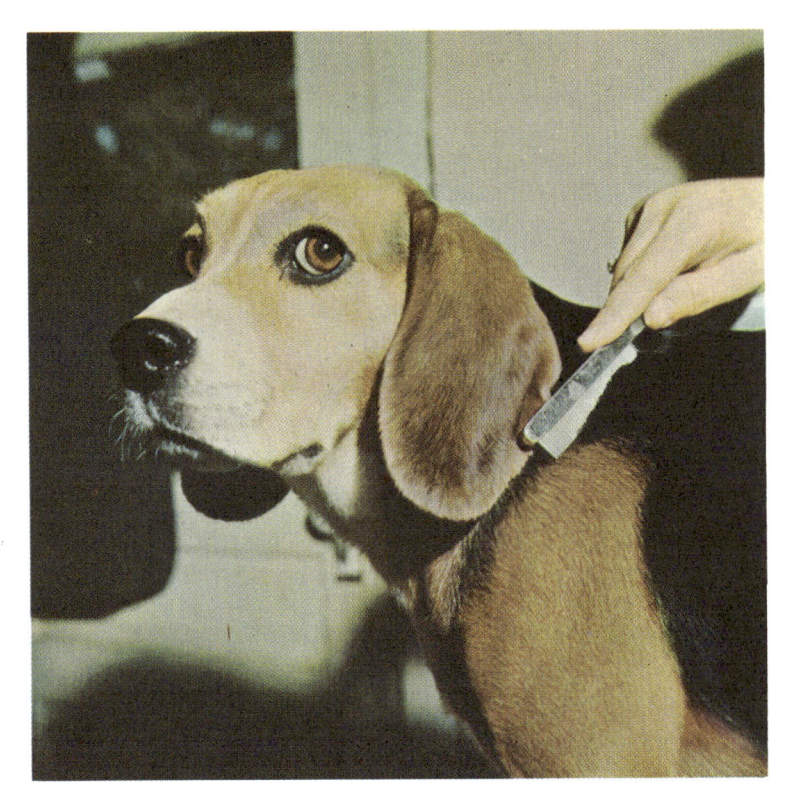

Regular grooming will keep a shine on your Beagle's coat and get rid of loose hair.

An older, experienced dog is the greatest help in training your Beagle. Your puppy will undoubtedly find the scent of a rabbit trail exciting, but he won't know what to do about it until he sees a rabbit jump up in front of him and sets sail in hot pursuit. With an older hound as guide he will learn the intricacies of working out a complex trail.

Accustoming your puppy to the gun is an important step. If you fire it at a distance at first, gradually decreasing the distance as he grows used to the sound, he will not be bothered by it. Do not actually shoot a rabbit he is driving until he is working well, and you can aim and be sure of a kill. Then he will be surprised at the connection of gun and dead bunny, but not frightened.

Beaglers are friendly people, and you will be able to learn much from more experienced trainers about handling your dog. In time you will learn about the finer points of handling and training, and may become interested in field trials. Your first Beagle probably will not be of champion caliber, but you can still enjoy hunting with him and learn much toward future trials. Most clubs hold fun trials, with dogs running in braces on cottontail or in packs on hare, as well as sanctioned and championship point trials. You will find them thrilling sports, whether you are competitor or spectator.

6. Caring for the Female and Raising Puppies

Whether or not you bought your female dog intending to breed her, some preparation is necessary when and if you decide to take this step.

WHEN TO BREED

It is usually best to breed on the second or third season. Plan in advance the time of year which is best for you, taking into account where the puppies will be born and raised. You will keep them until they are at least six weeks old, and a litter of husky pups takes up considerable space by then. Other considerations are selling the puppies (Christmas vs. springtime sales), your own vacation, and time available to care for them. You'll need at least an hour a day to feed and clean up after the mother and puppies but probably it will take you much longer — with time out to admire and play with them!

CHOOSING THE STUD

You can plan to breed your female about 6½ months after the start of her last season, although a variation of a month or two either way is not unusual. Choose the stud dog and make arrangements well in advance. If you are breeding for show stock, which may command better prices, a mate should be chosen with an eye to complementing the deficiencies of your female. If possible, the dogs should have several ancestors in common within the last two or three generations, as such combinations generally "click" best. The male should have a good show record or be the sire of show winners if old enough to be proven.

The owner of such a male usually charges a fee for the use of the dog. This does not guarantee a litter, but you generally have the right to breed your female again if she does not have puppies. In some cases the owner of the stud will agree to take a choice puppy in place of a stud fee. You should settle all details beforehand, including the possibility of a single surviving puppy, deciding the age at which he is to make his choice and take the pup, and so on.

If you want to raise a litter "just for the fun of it" and plan merely to

If their parents are healthy and friendly, the puppies are almost sure to turn out well.

make use of an available male, the most important selection point is temperament. Make sure the dog is friendly as well as healthy, because a bad disposition could appear in his puppies, and this is the worst of all traits in a dog destined to be a pet. In such cases a "stud fee puppy," not necessarily the choice of the litter, is the usual payment.

PREPARATION FOR BREEDING

Before you breed your female, make sure she is in good health. She should be neither too thin nor too fat. Any skin disease *must* be cured before it can be passed on to the puppies. If she has worms she should be wormed before being bred or within three weeks afterward. It is generally considered a good idea to revaccinate her against distemper and hepatitis before the puppies are born. This will increase the immunity the puppies receive during their early, most vulnerable period.

The female will probably be ready to breed 12 days after the first colored discharge. You can usually make arrangements to board her with the owner of the male for a few days, to insure her being there at the proper time, or you can take her to be mated and bring her home the same day. If she still appears receptive she may be bred again two days later. However, some females never show signs of willingness, so it helps to have the experience of a breeder. Usually the second day after the discharge changes color is the proper time, and she may be bred for about three days following. For an additional week or so she may have some discharge and attract other dogs by her odor, but can seldom be bred.

THE FEMALE IN WHELP

You can expect the puppies nine weeks from the day of breeding, although 61 days is as common as 63. During this time the female should receive normal care and exercise. If she was overweight, don't increase her food at first; excess weight at whelping time is bad. If she is on the thin side build her up, giving some milk and biscuit at noon if she likes it. You may add one of the mineral and vitamin supplements to her food to make sure that the puppies will be healthy. As her appetite increases, feed her more. During the last two weeks the puppies grow enormously and she will probably have little room for food and less appetite. She should be tempted with meat, liver and milk, however.

As the female in whelp grows heavier, cut out violent exercise and jumping. Although a dog used to such activities will often play with the children or run around voluntarily, restrain her for her own sake.

PREPARING FOR THE PUPPIES

Prepare a whelping box a few days before the puppies are due, and allow the mother to sleep there overnight or to spend some time in it during the day to become accustomed to it. Then she is less likely to try to have her pups under the front porch or in the middle of your bed. A variety of places will serve, such as a corner of your cellar, garage, or an unused room. If the weather is warm, a large outdoor doghouse will do, well protected from rain or draft. A whelping box serves to separate mother and puppies from visitors and other distractions. The walls should be high enough to restrain the puppies, yet allow the mother to get away from the puppies after she has fed them. Three feet square is minimum size, and six-inch walls will keep the pups in until they begin to climb, when the walls should be built up. Then the puppies really need more room anyway, so double the space with a very low partition down the middle and you will find them naturally housebreaking themselves.

Layers of newspaper spread over the whole area will make excellent bedding and be absorbent enough to keep the surface warm and dry. They should be removed daily and replaced with another thick layer. An old quilt or washable blanket makes better footing for the nursing puppies than slippery newspaper during the first week, and is softer for the mother.

Be prepared for the actual whelping several days in advance. Usually the female will tear up papers, refuse food and generally act restless. These may be false alarms; the real test is her temperature, which will drop to below 100° about 12 hours before whelping. Take it with a rectal thermometer morning and evening, and when the temperature goes down put her in the pen, looking in on her frequently.

WHELPING

Usually little help is needed but it is wise to stay close to make sure that the mother's lack of experience does not cause an unnecessary accident. Be ready to help when the first puppy arrives, for it could smother if the mother does not break the membrane enclosing it. She should start right away to lick the puppy, drying and stimulating it, but you can do it with a soft rough towel instead. The afterbirth should follow the birth of each puppy, attached to the puppy by the long umbilical cord. Watch to make sure that each is expelled, for retaining this material can cause infection. In her instinct for cleanliness the mother will probably eat the afterbirth after biting the cord. One or two will not hurt her; they stimulate milk supply as well as labor for remaining pups. But too many can make her lose appetite for the food she needs to feed her pups and regain her strength. So remove the rest of them along with the wet newspapers and keep the pen dry and clean to relieve her anxiety.

If the mother does not bite the cord, or does it too close to the body, take over the job, to prevent an umbilical hernia. Tearing is recommended, but you can cut it, about two inches from the body, with a sawing motion of scissors that have been sterilized in alcohol. Then dip the end of the cord in a shallow dish of iodine; the cord will dry up and fall off in a few days.

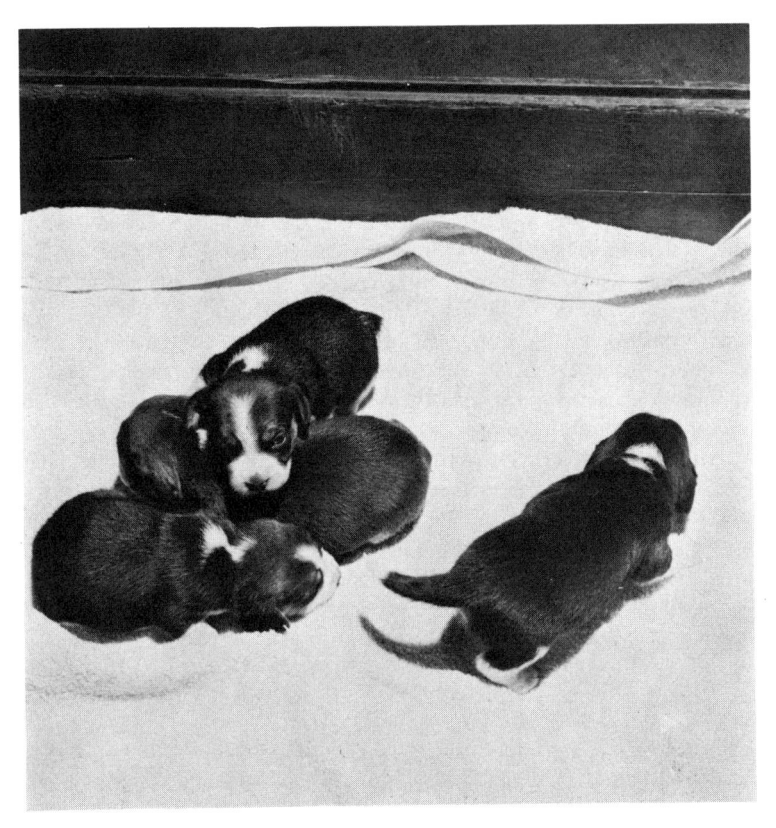

These healthy little Beagle puppies, their eyes newly opened, are just beginning to walk at weaning age.

The puppies should follow each other at intervals of not more than half an hour. If more time goes past and you are sure there are still pups to come, a brisk walk outside may start labor again. If your dog is actively straining without producing a puppy it may be presented backward, a so-called "breech" or upside-down birth. Careful assistance with a well-soaped finger to feel for the puppy or ease it back may help, but never attempt to pull it by force against the mother. This could cause serious damage, so let an expert handle it.

If anything seems wrong, waste no time in calling your veterinarian who can examine her and if necessary give hormones which will bring the remaining puppies. You may want his experience in whelping the litter even if all goes well. He will probably prefer to have the puppies born at his hospital rather than to get up in the middle of the night to come to your home. The mother would, no doubt, prefer to stay at home, but you can be sure she will get the best of care in his hospital. If the puppies are born at home and all goes as it should, watch the mother carefully afterward. It is wise to have the veterinarian check her and the pups, anyway, and remove the puppies' dewclaws.

RAISING THE PUPPIES

Hold each puppy to a breast as soon as he is dry, for a good meal without competition. Then he may join his littermates in a basket out of his mother's way while she is whelping. Keep a supply of evaporated milk on hand for emergencies, or later weaning. A formula of evaporated milk, corn syrup and a little water with egg yolk should be warmed and fed in a doll or baby bottle if necessary. A supplementary feeding often helps weak pups over the hump. Keep track of birth weights, and take weekly readings thereafter for an accurate record of the pups' growth and health.

After the puppies have arrived, take the mother outside for a walk and drink, and then leave her to take care of them. She will probably not want to stay away more than a minute or two for the first few weeks. Be sure to keep water available at all times, and feed her milk or broth frequently, as she needs liquids to produce milk. Encourage her to eat by giving her her favorite foods, until she asks for food of her own accord. She will soon develop a ravenous appetite and should have at least two large meals a day, with dry food available in addition.

Prepare a warm place to put the puppies to keep them dry and help them to a good start in life. You can use a cardboard box in which you put an electric heating pad or hot water bottle covered with flannel. Set the box near the mother so that she can see her puppies. She will usually allow you to help, but don't take the puppies out of sight. Let her handle things if your interference seems to make her nervous.

Be sure that all the puppies are getting enough to eat. If the mother sits or stands instead of lying still to nurse, the probable cause is scratching from the puppies' nails. You can remedy this by clipping them, as you do hers. Manicure scissors will do for these tiny claws.

Some breeders advise disposing of the smaller or weaker pups in a large litter, since the mother has trouble in handling more than six or seven. But you can help her out by preparing an extra puppy box or basket. Leave half the litter with the mother and the other half in a warm place, changing off at two-hour intervals at first. Later you may change the pups less frequently, leaving them all together except during the day. Try supplementary feeding, too; as soon as their eyes open, at about two weeks, they will lap from a dish, anyway.

WEANING THE PUPPIES

The puppies should normally be completely weaned at five weeks, although you start to feed them at three weeks. They will find it easier to lap semi-solid food than to drink milk at first, so mix baby cereal with whole or evaporated milk, warmed to body temperature, and offer it to the puppies in a saucer. Until they learn to lap, it is best to feed one or two at a time, because they are more likely to walk into it than to eat. Hold the saucer at chin level, and let them gather around, keeping paws out of the dish. A damp sponge afterward prevents most of the cereal from sticking to their skin if the mother doesn't clean them up. Once they have gotten the idea, broth or babies' meat soup may be alternated with milk, and you can start them on finely chopped meat. At four weeks they will eat four meals a day, and soon do without their mother entirely. Start them on mixed dog food, or leave it with them in a dish for self-feeding. Don't leave water with them all the time; at this age everything is to play with and they will use it as a wading pool. They can drink all they need if it is offered several times a day, after meals.

As the puppies grow up the mother will go into the pen only to nurse them, first sitting up and then standing. To dry her up completely, keep her away from the puppies for longer periods; after a few days of part-time nursing she can stay away for still longer periods, and then completely. The little milk left will be resorbed.

The puppies may be put outside, unless it is too cold, as soon as their eyes are open, and will benefit from the sunlight and vitamins. Provide a box with a rubber mat or newspapers on the bottom to protect them from cold or damp. At six weeks they can go outside permanently unless it is very cold, but make sure that they go into their shelter at night or in bad weather. By now cleaning up is a man-sized job, so put them out at least during the day and make your task easier. Be sure to clean their run daily, as worms and other infections are lurking. You can expect the pups to need at least one worming before they are ready to go to new homes, so take a stool sample to your veterinarian before they are three weeks old. If one puppy has worms all should be wormed. Follow the veterinarian's advice, and this applies also to vaccination. If you plan to keep a pup you will want to vaccinate him at the earliest age, so his littermates should be done at the same time.

7. Showing Your Beagle

As your puppy grows he will doubtless have many admirers among your friends, some of whom are bound to say, "Oh, what a handsome dog—you should certainly show him!" Perhaps even a breeder or judge will say he has show possibilities, and although you didn't buy him with that thought in mind, "Cinderella" champions do come along now and then—often enough to keep dog breeders perennially optimistic.

If you do have ideas of showing your dog, get the opinion of someone with experience first. With favorable criticism, go ahead with your plans to show him. For the novice dog and handler, sanction shows are a good way to gain ring poise and experience. These are small shows often held by the local kennel club or breed specialty club. Entry fees are low and paid at the door, breeds and sexes are usually judged together, and the prizes and ribbons are not important. They provide a good opportunity to learn what goes on at a show, and to conquer ring nervousness. Matches are usually held during the evening or on a weekend afternoon, and you need stay only to be judged.

Before you go to a show your dog should be trained to gait at a trot beside you, with head up and in a straight line. In the ring you will have to gait around the edge with other dogs and then individually up and down the center runner. In addition the dog must stand for examination by the judge, who will look at him closely and feel his head and body structure. He should be taught to stand squarely, hind feet slightly back, head and tail up on the alert. He must hold the pose when you place his feet and show animation for a piece of boiled liver in your hand or a toy mouse thrown in front of you.

ADVANCE PREPARATION

The day before the benched point show, pack your kit. You will want to take a water dish and bottle of water for your dog (so that he won't be affected by a change in drinking water, and you won't have to go look for it). Also take a chain or leash to fasten him to the bench or stall where he must remain during the show, and a show lead, as well as grooming tools. The show lead is a thin nylon or cord collar and leash combined, which does not detract from the dog's appearance as much as a clumsier chain and lead. Also put in the identification ticket sent by the show superintendent,

When you prepare your Beagle for the show ring, train him to pose like this excellent specimen.

noting the time you must be there and place where the show will be held, as well as time of judging.

If you have kept your dog's coat in good condition by weekly grooming, there is little to do the day before the show. Groom him thoroughly, clean the dog's teeth and if necessary wash his feet and legs if the dirt cannot be brushed out.

Entries close about two weeks in advance for the larger or "point" shows. You can obtain the dates of coming shows in your vicinity by writing to the Gaines Dog Research Center, 250 Park Ave., New York 17, N. Y. You will probably want to enter your dog in novice class, or in puppy class if he is between six and twelve months.

Don't feed your dog the morning of the show, or give him at most a light meal. He will be more comfortable in the car on the way, and will show more enthusiastically. When you arrive at the show grounds an official veterinarian will check your dog for health, and then you should find his bench and settle him there.

THE SHOW

Take your dog to the exercise ring to relieve himself, and give him a final grooming, then wait at the ring for your class to be called. All male classes are first, in this order: puppy, novice, bred by exhibitor. American-bred, open.

The winners compete for Winners Dog, who is awarded points toward his championship according to the number present. The winner competes

Trim your Beagle's whiskers close to his face for a neat appearance, but be very careful with the scissors.

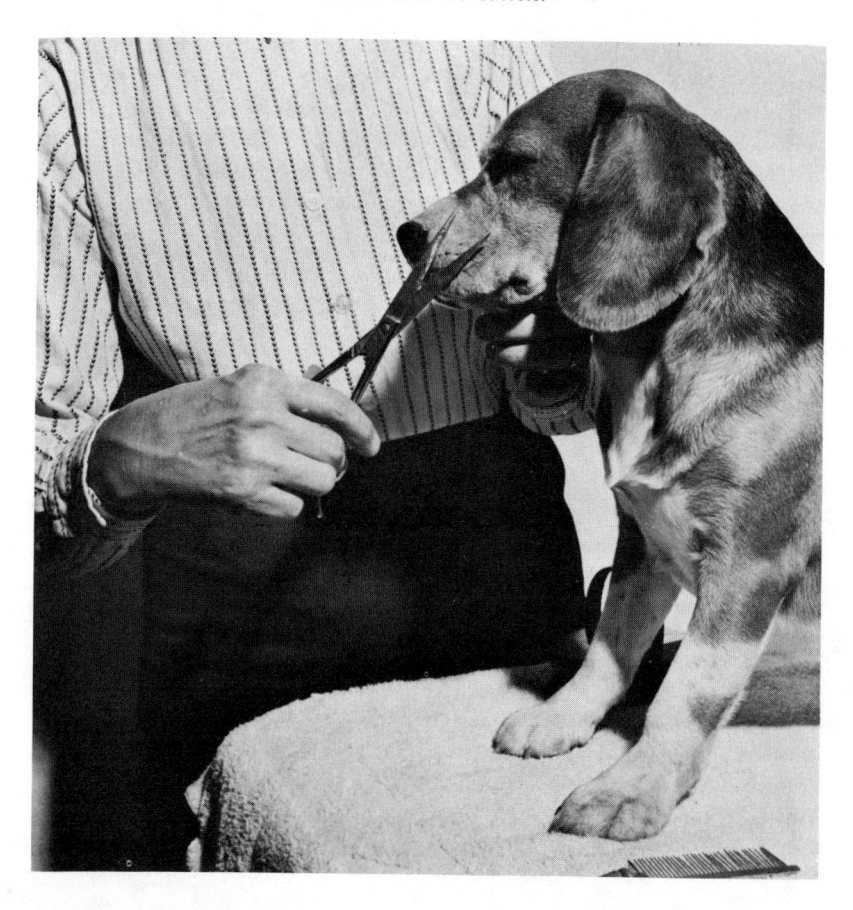

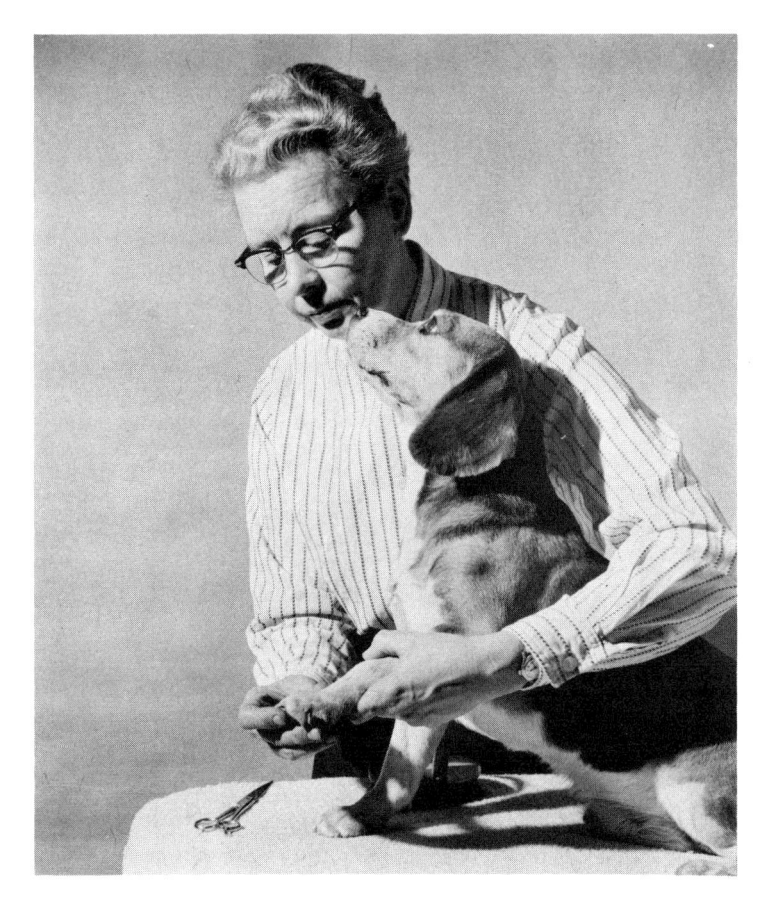

Trim the hair between your Beagle's toes, as well as his nails, so that he will have neat feet.

against the best female, then against champions entered in "specials only" for best of breed. The next step is the Hound group, where the best Beagle will compete against other hounds, including Afghans and Dachshunds, and the winner there goes on to try for best in show against Sporting, Working, Terrier Toy and Non-Sporting winners.

Another aspect of dog shows is the obedience trial. Any purebred dog may compete, to be judged on performance instead of conformation. There are three classes of increasing difficulty: novice, open and utility, leading to the degrees of C.D., C.D.X. and U.D.—companion dog (excellent) and utility dog. Tracking, or trailing, tests are also held.

If your dog has received the training we have described previously, he is well on the way to the necessary requirements for the novice class, and you may wish to continue. There are many obedience classes where an experienced trainer can help you with your dog; classes are held weekly at a nominal fee. It helps to accustom the dog to behaving in the company of others, but a daily training period at home is also necessary. For the novice class your dog must heel on and off leash, stand for examination, come when called, sit with you at the end of the ring for one minute, and lie down for three minutes. In advanced trials, retrieving, jumps, longer stays, and more difficult tasks are added. Attending an obedience class is excellent training for the show ring, or for a well-behaved dog you will be proud to own.

Appendix

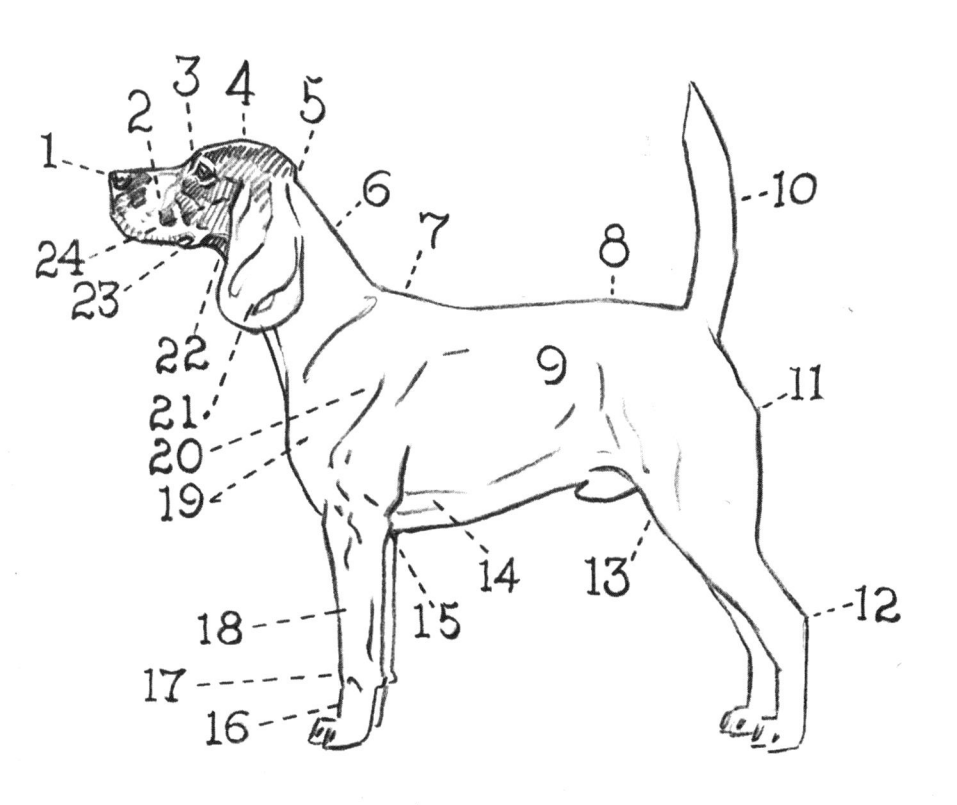

Parts of the Dog

1. Nose.
2. Muzzle.
3. Stop.
4. Skull.
5. Occiput.
6. Arch or Crest.
7. Withers or Top of Shoulders.
8. Hip.
9. Loin.
10. Brush or Flag.
11. Point of Rump.
12. Hock.
13. Stifle.
14. Chest.
15. Elbow.
16. Pastern.
17. Knee.
18. Forearm.
19. Point of Shoulder.
20. Shoulder.
21. Ear or Leather.
22. Dewlap.
23. Lips or Flews.
24. Cheek.

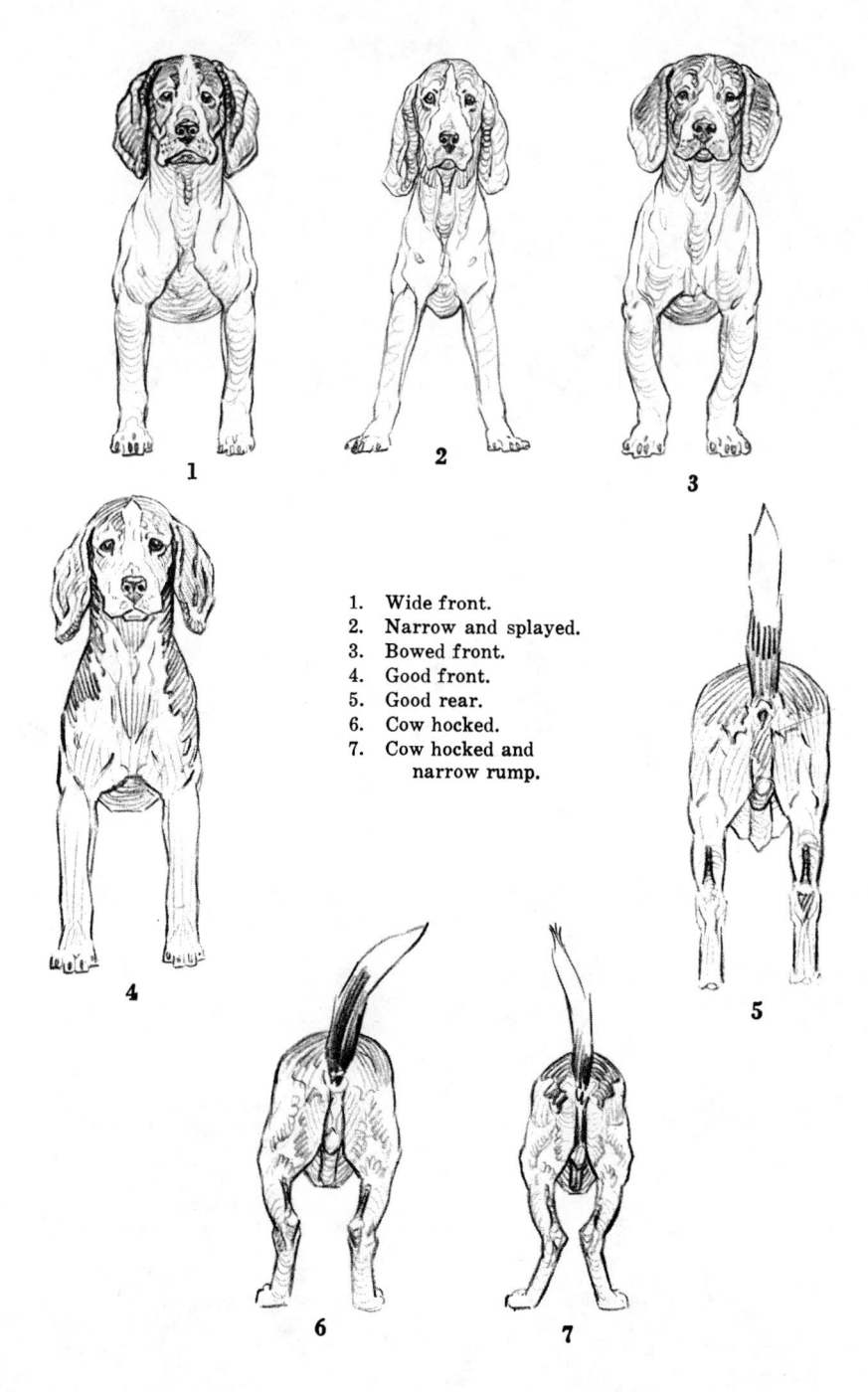

1. Wide front.
2. Narrow and splayed.
3. Bowed front.
4. Good front.
5. Good rear.
6. Cow hocked.
7. Cow hocked and narrow rump.

Heads

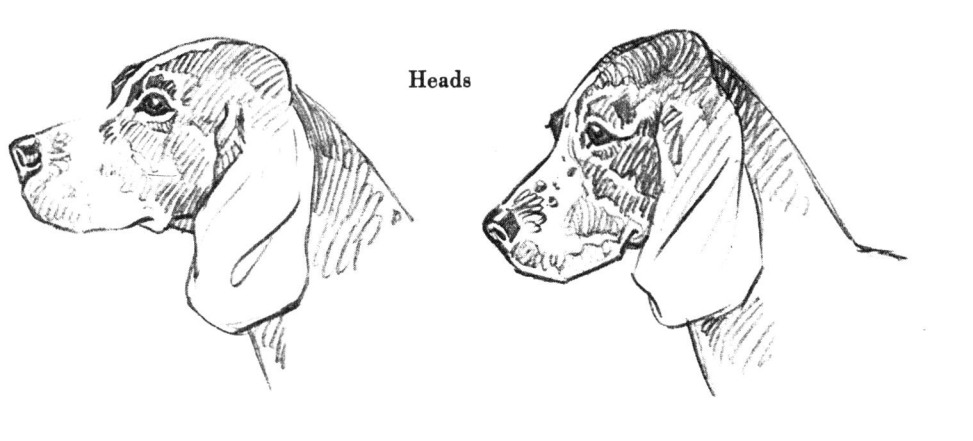

Good Head   Poor Head

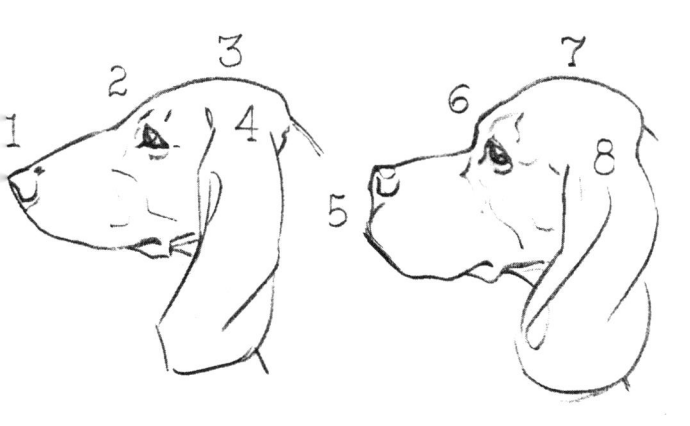

1. Snipey
2. Plain, lack of stop
3. Flat skull
4. High ear set
5. Coarse in muzzle
6. Too pronounced stop
7. Apple-domed
8. Short skull

9. Apple-domed
10, 11. High-set ears
12. Narrow skull
13. Too much lip
14. Flat skull
15. Snipey muzzle

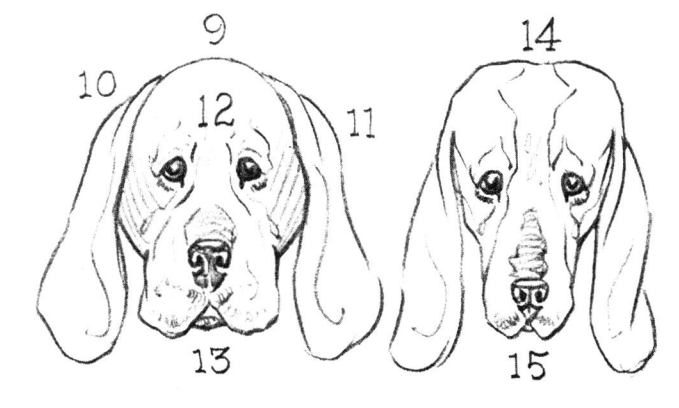

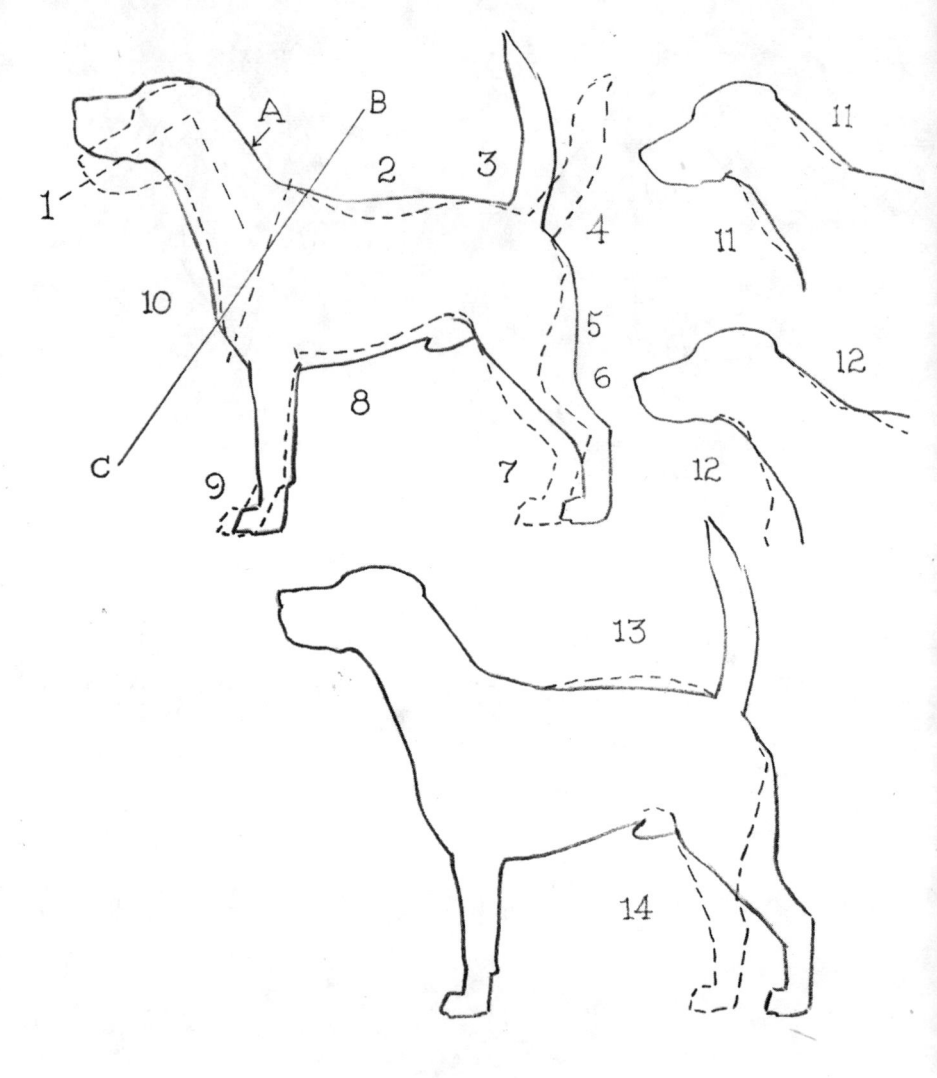

Good and Bad Profiles

Dotted lines indicate faulty profile, solid lines good profile.

1. Head set on badly
2. Sway-backed
3. Low tail set
4. Tail too crooked
5, 6, 7. Weak rear
8. Shallow chest
9. Weak pastern
10. Upright shoulder
11. Ewe-neck
12. Short neck
13. Roach-backed
14. Stifle too straight
A. Good crest line of neck
B.-C. Good slope of shoulder

Good Mover — Side View

This hound has a good free-reaching effortless stride that eats up the ground. Note (below) the space between A-B and C-D as the dog stretches out to front and rear. This is possible because the shoulders, elbows, hips, and stifles are properly placed and angulated, and so permit free movement under the chest and loins.

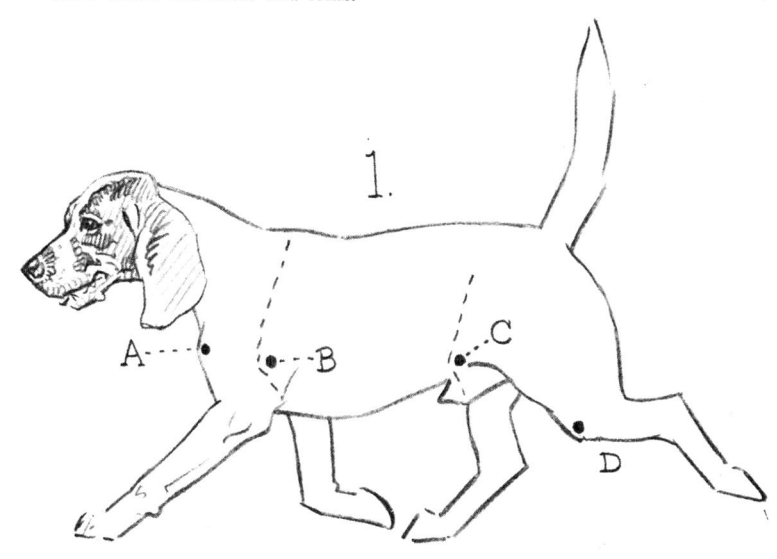

Beagle turning left handed while running hard

A-1 is a good mover. He is on the proper lead, i.e., he is landing on his *right* fore foot. The left will be the second to hit the ground. B-1 is a poor mover. He will not have the balance or finesse of movement that A-1 will have. B-1 is in the same phase of stride but he is landing on the left fore foot.

A-2 shows the good mover on his left fore foot which is more under his center of balance. B-2 being on wrong lead does not have the support under his center of balance for the turn.

A good dog like a good horse *must* move on the proper lead.